A Journal of Love and Healing

Transcending Grief

Sylvia Browne

and

Nancy Dufresne

Hay House, Inc.
Carlsbad, California • Sydney, Australia

Published and distributed in the United States by:
Hay House, Inc., P.O. Box 5100, Carlsbad, CA 92018-5100
(800) 654-5126 • (800) 650-5115 (fax)

Editorial Supervision: Jill Kramer   Cover Design: Christy Salinas

Library of Congress Cataloging-in-Publication Data

Browne, Sylvia.
  A journal of love and healing : transcending grief / by Sylvia Browne and Nancy Dufresne.
      p. cm.
  ISBN 1-56170-808-9 (trade)
  1. Death—Miscellanea. 2. Grief—Miscellanea. 3. Spiritualism. I. Dufresne, Nancy. II. Title.

BF1275.D2 B76 2001
133.9—dc21

                                                  00-063244

                      ISBN 1-56170-808-9

              04 03 02 01   4 3 2 1
                  1st printing, February 2001

        Printed in China Through Palace Press International

Contents

Acknowledgments

To all the people I love, and to all who love me.

— Sylvia Browne

❊ ❊ ❊

To my parents, who taught me that love and honesty are the true treasures that last forever; and for giving me integrity and a strong foundation to seek my own destiny and learn my own lessons with pride and conviction.

To my insightful and loving husband, for sharing his strength and his softness.

To my son, for saving me by letting me see the world again through a child's eyes.

To a couple of phenomenal friends who have continued to care for my heart at times when I was unable to do it for myself, and who have loved me when I had nothing to give back.

To Sylvia, for loving me as part of her family at first sight, and for years of amazing experiences that she has shared with me. I especially acknowledge her for walking this path with me, and for believing in me enough to be a part of this message that I have wanted to share with others.

— Nancy Dufresne

*I*n the book of Ruth, the story explains that Naomi's sons each married. One married Orpah and one married Ruth. Both men died, leaving Orpah and Ruth widowed, and Naomi without her sons. The book of Ruth is a story of love, devotion, common bonds, and shared grief.

Ruth 1:15: "See," Naomi said to her, "your sister-in-law has gone back to her people and to her gods; you should do the same."

Ruth 1: 16–17: But Ruth replied, "Don't make me leave you, for I want to go wherever you go, and to live wherever you live; your people shall be my people, and your God shall be my God; I want to die where you die, and be buried there. May the Lord do terrible things to me if I allow anything but death to separate us."

Ruth 1:18: And when Naomi saw that Ruth had made up her mind and could not be persuaded otherwise, she stopped urging her.

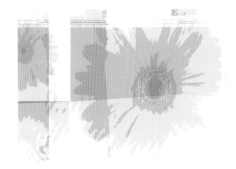

Preface

By Sylvia Browne

My daughter-in-law Nancy and I decided to write this journal not only because she and I have lived almost 20 years of our lives together, but also because we have a unique relationship on many levels.

First, I love her as a daughter, far beyond the fact that she is married to my first-born beloved son, Paul. Our lives seem to run on so many parallel tracks. It is unique in life to find souls who are meshed together, but it is extra special in this society to find a mother and daughter-in-law who are so close.

I won't go into all of the other levels that show how similar we are, because this is a journal dedicated to transcending the grief that arises after loved ones pass. Sometimes I call it the last frontier, because for all of us, death is the pinnacle of human emotion. Death is the joy of graduation for those who have gone before, but here in this journal, we are addressing those of us who are left behind.

Because I am a psychic and am privileged to receive an infusion of information from the Other Side, I can and will take the spiritual voice. This mantle is a part of me that cannot be separated from my own skin or essence—because of what I *know*, and don't just *believe*—to be the truth. Yes, I can assure you that those who have already passed have not only made it to the Other Side, but are in a state of bliss.

Knowing this fact makes us happy, and yet sad. We often find ourselves in a black hole of despair. At first, we can find little solace in the fact that "they" may be under a tree in a beautiful meadow with all their loved ones who have gone before them. It is simply no comfort to us at that moment that they can see us and watch over us. We feel this way because they are not with us. Here we are, alone, left to manage without them. We often feel very guilty for having all of these feelings. It's confusing. We feel bad because they're gone, and we want them to be here with us no matter how wonderful the Other Side is.

Alfred Lord Tennyson, in his "In Memoriam," addressed the stages of grief and said that there's about a 100 percent probability that you'll go through all of them at some time in your life: the disbelief, the despair, the denial, the anger, the resentment, and even the whys and hows.

Why me? How can God let this happen?

But through all these steps, eventually you'll learn many

lessons, and your spirituality will grow, and then comes the absolute *knowing* that you and your loved ones will be together again.

❈ ❈ ❈

By Nancy Dufresne

This journal of love and healing is a creation stemming from intense love, a sense of loss, and the need for certainty that we can continue our relationships with those who have gone "Home." It is a tangible way in which we can maintain a loving bond with those who have taken part in our common journey.

For me, this journal came about as a result of a shared moment that made time stand still. One day as Sylvia and I sat by the sea, frozen with sadness about our deceased loved ones, I realized that I could no longer run from the overwhelming sense of loss and grief. It was clear to me that I must run to it and pull it close to me—to take from it whatever would help me move forward into life's continued adventures.

I knew, without a doubt, that it was also a matter of survival, a path that I had no choice but to pursue. In those moments by the sea, I faced my anger with the world because it did not stop, not even for a second, when either one of my parents died. The world changed drastically for *me* because they left, and it was also forever changed because they had *lived.* That knowledge gave me the courage to face reality slowly, because I was living in a world that my parents had a hand in creating and changing, and I'm proud of them. I also wanted to play a part in creating and changing the world for all of those I love and empathize with.

All of this happened in those precious moments by the sea as Sylvia and I shared the deepest sensations of pain and love. The unspoken words between us could have filled volumes, and ultimately led us in this direction.

Through this journal, we are embracing you and understanding all your pain and sharing your sorrow. Know that you will not be walking alone down that dark hallway. Open your mind and open your heart, and allow your spirit to walk with ours on the path laid before you. Many tears will be shed, and you will find yourself smiling or even laughing from time to time while remembering and sharing your life through your reflections. This is a precious communication with yourself, with us, and with those who have gone Home before us.

This journal is a way to embrace grief and be proud that you're a loving person who feels so deeply. This is a way to gain the knowledge and character that you might not have otherwise found on another path. We were not meant to *get over* someone we have loved. We were meant to cultivate the loss and plant it like a seed, one that will someday bear fruit or bring forth a sweet flower and add beauty to our lives and those lives we touch.

We all have a purpose—every action in life has a purpose—and so, too, does dying and being the one left behind.

Those of us who find our way through the fear and pain have accomplished much as part of both a learning and teaching process.

The journey of grief has many turns, so let this be your safe place to express yourself honestly and completely. So from our hearts to yours, we bring you *A Journal of Love and Healing*. May it help you transcend your grief and achieve contentment and peace of mind.

❄ ❄ ❄ ❄ ❄ ❄

This is something I wrote for Sylvia with my love, compassion, gratitude, and understanding shortly after we spoke with our hearts and souls by the sea.

— **Nancy**

Lost in the Night, Found by the Sea

In the quietness of the night, I felt a chill. Pulling the comforter up close to my face, I felt no comfort.

My heartbeat sounded different. There was an echo that rang in my ears; it sounded like loneliness.

As I clenched my hands over my ears to stop the sound, I found myself powerless to change what certainly was.

I wrapped my arms tightly around my chest, but my arms could not mimic the arms I ached for.

I looked into the shadows and wondered, Who will recognize the young girl hiding in my eyes? Who will understand the story in my sighs? Will anyone notice that my laugh is not as deep or as true as it once had been, or that my smile had a hidden grimace to it?

Would there be a place for my heart to feel at home again? I wondered where to look for someone who could touch my hand, and in that simple human contact, make the living grief that nested inside of me go to sleep for just a little while. Whose eyes could I meet that would know the strengths in my pain rather than the weakness? Where is someone who has a tear streaming slowly down her cheek that matches mine, a tear that has traveled the same path?

As panic took my breath, I threw the comfortless comforter aside and reached out for someone who was no longer there. Feeling my hand on the phone, my breathing quick and shallow, reality seared my senses, there was NOBODY HOME!

Forcing my body up, I turned on the light, hoping that the brightness would give me perspective and courage; it did not.

I moved in front of the mirror and studied my face. I did not recognize myself; I was just a little girl, much too small and still in need of loving protection, encouragement, and guidance to have this face, this adult face. I wanted to call out; they always came when I was scared, yet I knew no one would be coming anymore.

So as I stared into my own eyes searching for "them," I caught a brief glimpse, but it gave me more longing and anger than comfort and peace. I slid down to the floor, letting my hand trail the wall to extinguish the light and the reality I saw in the mirror.

I pulled my knees to my chest and locked my hands around them as if to wear armor, only to find it futile. In the darkness, I crawled, like a baby, groping for my bed and any fragments of answers that might be hiding in the night.

Then in the stillness, something surrounded me, something soft and welcome. It came in waves, in constant, rhythmic motion. With my eyes wide open, I could see a slight stream of flickering light creeping in through the shutters. While I stared at that thin thread of dancing light, I remembered a moment when I was sitting by the sea. I remembered feeling pulled into the ocean's vast mysterious essence and remembered how my searching warm brown eyes suddenly filled with tears sent directly from my heart. The little girl lost cried out in silent frantic panic. The orphan child I had become lifted her head to see a most precious sight. I saw another child searching in grief. Her beautiful, soulful brown eyes also welled with tears. I could hear her heart scream and feel the anguish that pulled at her. I could see what a brave little girl she had become and recognize the fears that lay unspoken on her face.

Then she encircled me with her arms, the arms of a child welcoming comfort, the arms of a strong woman and loving mother, the arms of a friend and kindred soul. For one perfect moment, our hearts and our eyes spoke. Our grief found the open door that led us to a safe place, a place to be that person we so often had to hide, a place that we created, the place that gave us each other to reach out for, and a place that felt like home.

So when the night visitor comes again, as it surely will, to bring its gnawing questions and emptiness, when it brings me longings for what once was, and the fear of losing myself without anyone noticing, when I cannot find home, I will look for your open door. When the visitor reminds me of how I ache for a safe place to rest my heart and a warm connection to a trusted soul, I will remember your touch and your tears.

When the visitor comes to you in the night and you feel lost, remember that I, too, give the same precious refuge to your heart as you have given mine. When the visitor comes for us, let us look away from its unwelcome familiar face and, instead, remember our moment sitting by the sea.

❋ ❋ ❋ ❋ ❋ ❋

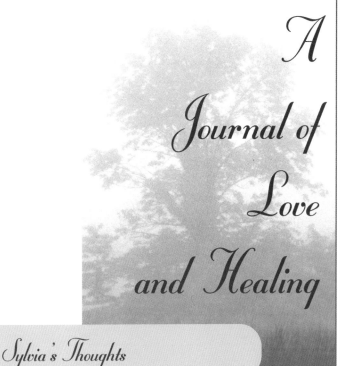

A Journal of Love and Healing

Sylvia's Thoughts

Realization

There are times when I cannot eat, sleep, or complete a clear thought. It is a comfort knowing that this is a "normal" and temporary state of being for a person traveling the road of grief into a future of deeper love, understanding, and spiritual evolvement.

I lost nine people in about four months. The most painful was my father; losing my mother was less painful.

Nancy lost both her beloved mother and her strict but loving father only a few years later. This is by no means to say that anyone's grief is harder than anyone else's. A death of a child is, I feel, the hardest, but even then it's all relative in the scheme of living and loving. The one thing we all share—and it *does* make us sisters and brothers under the skin—is the devastation that attacks all of us.

With all the commonality that Nancy and I have gone through, we were drawn even closer by the realization that no matter what age we were, both of us were orphans. No one would remember what we remembered. The elders that stood as protective shields, as references to our past, and reflections of who we were and are and where we came from, were gone.

We had become the elders. This isn't by any means related to age, only the positioning of the chess pieces in this game called Life. We had been checkmated, and we had no choice but to submit and ride that dark horse down into the depths of our own tears, memories, and longings.

How this began to materialize was that I had just come off a 66-city tour and decided that my son, Paul; Nancy; and my precious grandson, Jeffrey, should take off for a week in Hawaii. I hadn't taken any time off for almost 20 years until the last few after Mama and Daddy died—partly because I couldn't afford it, and partly because I'm so involved with my work.

One evening in October of 1999, right around my birthday, we had gone to a beautiful place to eat, right by the ocean in Maui. I had gotten up from the table and walked toward the ocean and sat down looking out at the setting sun and the azure sea. As it so often does, the full impact of grief hit me. Within seconds, Nancy was sitting beside me, silent. We were both silent. We looked out over the vastness of the ocean and drew physically closer, literally leaning on each other for support. We put our arms around each other, and as we turned our heads to face each other, our eyes spoke volumes. Our hearts heard the breaking of each other's hearts and heard the emptiness that the loss had left inside of us. Few words were spoken, many tears fell, and everything was understood.

Sometimes, just when you think the dragon has gone to sleep, without warning it awakens with its howling mouth agape, and its fire that spews out takes your breath away. It's the dragon that sleeps deep in your gut that is called *grief*.

It will awaken all the time in the beginning of your descent into the hell of your loss. As time goes on, the dragon frequently goes to sleep, only to arise with a vengeance. It causes memories to fly into your mind, and there's nothing that can stop it.

I see the memories of dear friends, such as my friend, Dr. Small; and I see my dearest Daddy, his distinct laugh, and his sparkle of pride for whatever I did. I see it all flash in my mind. I see the memories of Warren, Chris, Marvin, William, Ada, Marcus, Celeste, Milly—and the list goes on and on. The faces, places, and times; the hugs and laughter; and of course, the pain of their loss, surrounds me. Then I feel the stillness with its own flavor and demons.

In the stillness, you can hear your own heart beating and sometimes curiously wonder, *Why does it still beat? Didn't my heart break into a million pieces, so how can it still be heard and felt?* Then in those moments, you begin to come just an inch closer to perfection. You realize that your heart beats for you and for God and for all of the people you love. Your heart beats until you've learned the lesson that there *is* a greater plan.

Realization

There are some issues that may seem too raw to address, but the sooner we can get a grip on this illness called grief, then the sooner we will stay focused and not allow it to overtake us. It is not a cure-all, but it helps to address and explore grief and learn its personality. Knowledge is power— take it from us; we know.

Exercise

We tend to transfer our pain from loss to a part of our body. This exercise is to help you identify and release the part or parts of your body that are being affected by the emotional pain of the grieving process.

Put your right hand *immediately* on whatever part of your body comes to mind when you read the word *grief*.

Keep your hand on the affected area, and take a very slow, deep breath.

Now let it out in a big sigh.

Begin to feel the tightness and tension in that area leaving you.

Keeping your hand on the same area, take in another slow, deep breath. Now let it out with a loud groan, as loud as you want.

Do it one more time in the same manner.

The areas of your body that are taking in the emotional pain and transferring it to physical pain will begin to release and relax.

Continue to practice this exercise daily or nightly until you feel your body's physical reaction to grief dissipating.

Realization

The quicker you allow your mind to accept and be conditioned to the idea that you can see and communicate with those on the Other Side, the easier your journey will be. Don't make it hard. As I have often said in lectures or on TV, our loved ones who have gone to the Other Side are only a breath away.

Notes for Reflection

_____

_____

_____

_____

_____

_____

_____

Nancy's Thoughts

Beginnings and endings are so similar. Each is the start of an unknown journey, yet both are equally important and are journeys we have no choice but to take.

Learning to live with the death of a person or persons I love is teaching me more about myself and about living. I am more complex than I realized, and yet I'm honest about my weaknesses. I am in the process of learning that weakness is a strength, not a flaw. It is a bittersweet gift given to those of us who have earned it. Through my weakness, I build my path, yellow brick by yellow brick, living in a world that has changed forever, and one that will continue to be filled with unknowns. Through sorrow, I have grown to understand what is truly important. I have forgiven things I may not have prior to my loss, and I have come to truly know that in the end, love is all that we take Home.

Loss is all too familiar to me. Six days before my mother died, my paternal grandmother passed on. Days later after Mom died, Daddy and I felt emotionally bankrupt and dazed. We could barely face the gravity of pain in our hearts. As Daddy and I planned my mother's funeral and did all the chores that go along with that, we carried my then four-month-old son with us, faced with the beginning and end of life in the same moments.

Through our shared loss, Daddy and I began a relationship that we probably would have otherwise never known. We grew closer, becoming each other's bridge to the past, as well as each other's shoulder to lean on.

Daddy, though, was never quite the same after Mom died. He tried to be happy and move forward, but he got stuck in what he missed so deeply. His emotional and physical health suffered steadily.

In early July of the year Daddy died, my husband, Paul; our son, Jeffrey, Sylvia and her husband, Larry, and I went for a much-needed vacation in Mexico. I was restless, and my thoughts were home with Daddy.

One evening, I went and sat on the balcony. While listening to the waves crash against the rocks, I had a "talk" with my mother as I often did and still do. I asked Mom to help Daddy find more joy in life, to help him be healthier physically, and if that was not possible, to take him Home where he would be with her and out of emotional and physical pain. As soon as the words came out of my mouth, I felt guilty for the last part of my request.

I went back inside and stood by the kitchen window, feeling sad and even more guilty. Just then, Sylvia shouted, "Nancy, come here!" I ran into the other room expecting to see my son with a bump or scrape, and instead saw Sylvia pointing across the room.

She said, "The light just flickered on and off, and I just saw your mother walk by with the sweetest smile. She was wearing a light blue sweat suit outfit."

I had to sit down upon hearing that.

I had just asked Mom for help, and there she was, as always, at my side when I needed her. The amazing thing is that Sylvia described the blue sweat suit that my mother wore to a frazzle. I used to tease her, asking her if that was the only one she owned. She would just smile and say, "It's my favorite, and so comfy."

I still have that sweat suit in my dresser drawer.

Shortly after we returned home, Daddy went into a rapid physical and emotional decline. Here was my father, this strong man, who protected me and raised me in an old-fashioned, strict atmosphere, teaching me integrity and responsibility and so much more, and now he was dying before my eyes.

I felt that he was leaving me, too—the child inside of me was losing her way home. He raised me to be strong, and I feared that I would disappoint him because I was falling apart. The reality of it all paralyzed me.

I was afraid, since Daddy was my safety net. I just thought, *Oh no, not again. Not now, it's too soon. I won't survive.* Then I thought, *How selfish and narrow of me.* But I couldn't stop feeling increasing panic. Daddy died late that July.

I had promised him that he wouldn't die alone. I told him I would be there, and I just missed being with him, which also flooded me with guilt. I actually still haven't completely forgiven myself. When I arrived at the hospital and saw him lying still in his bed, I apologized for not being with him. Paul was waiting for me and was trying to help me deal with my guilt and pain, but all the love he gave me in those moments could not save me from the internal devastation that overcame me.

Losing my remaining parent was worse than I could have ever imagined in my worst nightmares. My heart *did* feel broken and hollow. I think I survived it initially because my husband and son gave me love and patience and allowed me my solitude for as long as I needed it (and sometimes still need). Sylvia and her husband, Larry, took my irrational and urgent phone calls at all times of the day or night and talked me through many panic attacks. I was also blessed with some precious people (you know who you are) who let me be a child and held me up so I could walk through the thick fog that surrounded me daily.

I felt as if I were seven years old, a small girl in the night calling for Daddy to watch me walk down the long dark hall, as he always did when I was a little girl. I would ask him, "Daddy can you see me? Are you watching me?" He always said, "Yes, I can see you. Daddy will make sure you're safe." I prayed that he was watching me then, that he would help me make it down that long dark hallway again, because I was so very scared. I still pray that he's watching me now.

When we become motherless, fatherless, childless, or widowed, the experience takes our breath away. We cannot find anywhere to go where we can make sense of our feelings. We turn around and around, trying to find the way out of the maze of loneliness in the aftermath of loss. The moment we lose someone who is a part of our heart, we are forever changed. That which does not kill us, in my opinion, defines who we become. Knowing that there is nothing that can change what has happened sends waves of panic and anxiety through our every cell and makes us feel fragmented. Even though we know the person we have loved and now lost in the physical realm is safe and happy on the Other Side, we want him or her to be here with us. We still want that relationship.

I have found that being an adult all the time is exhausting. Sometimes I just want to lay my head down so that someone will stroke my hair and tell me that everything will be all right. I am blessed that my husband, Paul; a dear girlfriend; and my precious mother-in-law, Sylvia, all give me unconditional love and understanding. My wish is that you, too, will feel that same degree of comfort as you go through this journal.

I have had many well-meaning people ask me, "Aren't you over this yet? Just pull yourself up and keep going."

I have never wasted time trying to push away my feelings. I *don't have to* pull myself up and be tough. How can you forget or get over someone who has filled your heart with unbelievable joy, someone whom you have loved and who has loved and cherished you—someone who has changed your life? It doesn't even make sense. It's too much to expect of a human being.

Realization

If my heart aches any more, I feel that it might explode. I stop and breathe deeply and slowly. I give myself permission to become familiar with the physical panic associated with my deep loss. I recognize it as a sign that I am alive, and a loving person. I close my eyes and think of you sitting across the table from me, smiling. Your smile has always given me great joy and comfort. I allow myself to be comforted by you now.

Notes for Reflection

Sylvia's Thoughts

I see the pain in Nancy's face as I do in my clients' faces. Of course I see Nancy more often than I see my clients, so I've become familiar with my dear daughter-in-law's dragon, as she has become familiar with mine. It *does* help to have a companion who is able to empathize with you even if there are no words to say. There is a sense of *knowing* between those of us who walk the uncertain path of grief. So as you write in your journal, you will find that we are not the only ones who are truly with you. God is your Guide, and your angels are beside you, giving you comfort. Even more important in this time of grief, your loved ones are certainly with you.

The other night, William, my two-and-a-half-year-old grandson, walked into my bedroom where I was sorting photos. I came across a picture of my dad. Sometimes we're able to look at pictures, and sometimes we're not. On this night,

I could look. Before I could hand the photo to Willie, he grabbed it and looked at Dad's picture. For a moment, Willie got a faraway look in his eyes, and then he said, "That's my girl."

No one ever said that to me but Daddy. It was his trademark phrase of encouragement and pride. I just stared, and then pulled myself together, realizing that William had heard my Dad's spirit voice tell him that phrase! At that moment, I saw my father's face next to Willie's for an instant.

No one always hears what I hear or sees what I see, which sometimes casts me into a form of isolation, but God knows, I would not trade any moment when a loved one breaks through.

As *you* move through your own journey, you will become aware of your loved ones breaking through and communicating with you. Keep your vision broad and your mind and heart open. Talk with them, write to them, and ask that they come to you. You will truly find that they will let you know that they are still with you.

Realization

Your pillow still smells like you. I love that smell. It brings me comfort, vivid memories, and a sense that you are all around me. It makes me realize that your personal touch and style and so much of you is still here with me. The smell of you gives me shelter, and now I can actually feel your presence and know that you're right next to me, giving me whatever it is I need in this moment.

Exercise

Lie down in a quite place and relax your body, beginning with your feet and moving upward to the top of your head.

Now see yourself in a field. The grass is very green, swaying in the light breeze. There are trees and colorful flowers everywhere. You may feel alone at first, but be patient; you'll begin to feel a presence around you. Some may be your angels or your spirit guides or both. Now ask your guide to bring your loved one to you. At first you may just get a feeling of a presence, but gradually, as you do this, your mind opens up.

Cutting through years of programming, be it cultural or religious, takes time. The more you do this—and it only takes a few moments—the more your loved ones will know that you're trying to reach them. They're just as anxious as we are to show you that the soul survives.

Notes for Reflection

_____

_____

_____

_____

_____

_____

_____

Nancy's Thoughts

I recall the very moment that I was told that my mother was terminally ill. I remember the sick feeling all over my body and the fog in my head. I remember the look on her face when she was told, and how she buried her head in my father's chest, as if trying to hide from the truth. Well, I tried to hide, too.

In that instant, I began to grieve the impending loss of my mother.

Throughout Mom's entire illness, I kept asking her not to leave me. "Don't go, Mom. It will be okay. The treatment will work. . . ." But she became weaker. As she lost strength, she still tried to comfort *me;* she tried to take away *my* fears. She told me that she was trying to stay for me; she didn't want to leave *me*, either. One day she told me that she just couldn't stay for me much longer, that the pain was overwhelming, yet I still fought the inevitable.

The night she died, I tried to stay in my denial and tell myself that it wasn't happening, not tonight. My husband, as gently as he could, looked at me with tears in his eyes and said, "You should go to the hospital. If you don't, I will. Face it, she's dying, and she shouldn't be alone."

My own tears fell freely, and I knew that his words were so true. I rushed to my car and to Mom's bedside. As I drove to the hospital, I was angry. She was not just my mother, but my friend, my ally, my safe place, my home. I had a four-month-old baby, so how dare she leave me now when I was a new mother and still needed to be mothered myself. After all, this was not how I'd planned it. Still, I knew that it was how it would be. The whole situation was out of my control. I could not stop this devastating loss.

When I got to Mom's room, I felt as though my senses were heightened. I remember every detail. I talked to her about my childhood and what she meant to me, and I said all the wonderful things I wanted to say. Then I physically felt a change in the atmosphere of the room. It was not just Mom and me any longer.

The air was thick, and I felt surrounded, insulated, and calm. I literally felt as if I were wrapped in cotton. I put my face next to my mother's and thought how wonderful it was that we were together, and what a privilege it was for me to be here when she was leaving this world. I felt as though someone's hands were on my shoulders, giving me courage and comfort.

I was then able to do the most unselfish thing I have ever done for my mother. I told Mom that I would be strong, that the baby and Paul would be fine, and that Daddy and I would take care of each other. I asked her to go Home, knowing that her love would always live inside me. I told Mom to look for the light, to look for her mother and father, and to be happy for all she left behind and all she was going to. Letting her go took all I had, and I was grateful for the strength that I found within me.

I felt peace and closure with my mother, unlike with Daddy. Being with Mom made me feel so complete in our relationship.

Still, after Mom and Daddy's deaths, I felt, and still do feel, anger. I feel a loneliness that is of no insult to anyone whom I love or who loves me; it's just an ache for what once was and what will never be. Every time there's a milestone in my family's life, I reach for the phone. I can't wait to tell Mom and Daddy. Every time I have a birthday, I want to hear the same story my mother told year after year about how she had to be induced to deliver me.

So you see, all of these things that some people may see as "carrying on" or "not getting over it" are just situations that those people don't understand. Actually, it's quite normal, and inspires more emotional and spiritual growth than simply forgetting about those we have lost. Grief *does* have a positive side and a purpose.

I am learning that I am still very much on the journey of my grief process, and I have not put a time limit on how long it will take me to travel this path. I am a fortunate woman, though, because I have a mother-in-law who not only touches my heart with her awareness of my pain and with her encouragement and strength; but who also has a powerful belief in me, in us, and in traveling this journey and coming out enriched by it.

I still remember what Sylvia said to me the very first time she saw me almost 20 years ago. She looked into my eyes, smiled, and said, "Now I know why Paul loves you." She still looks at me that way.

Being loved like that, knowing that no matter what mistakes I might make, there's still someone in my life who loves me as a mother does, is a feeling so precious and so comforting that words escape me.

Hearing Sylvia's words about her own personal grief and experiences, and seeing her as a woman and an "orphan child" as well as someone who offers words of spiritual growth and guidance, is a gift that I know will ease *your* pain as well.

Realization

As I ask for help, I learn to accept all that I'm feeling about the changes in my life. I ask to learn well so that I might share what you, my loved ones, continue to give me through our new way of communicating.

Notes for Reflection

_____

_____

_____

_____

_____

_____

_____

_____

_____

_____

_____

_____

_____

Sylvia's Thoughts

Let's backtrack a little. Before we came into this Earthly existence, we existed in a plane more real than this one. We existed before we were here, and we will exist again.

Prior to coming into this life, we began to chart out a schematic. We decided what type of life we were going to come into and what we were going to learn. Individually and collectively, we made these plans. And there isn't a single soul that makes a plan or chart without including other people.

For example, we may decide that we need to learn lessons A, B, and C, and contribute X to the world. We may also decide how fast we go through this life in the completion of our plan. We may decide that we will do this quickly, and that "Jane" or "Joe" will carry on with our contributions after we've gone Home.

Some people choose not to exit fast and to live longer, while others choose to make this a brief stay. Some of us even choose to go through the demise of a loved one. Then when we actually come into this life, we don't want to do it anymore.

We all have five exit points, or options, in our lifetime. Why do we have five? I asked Francine, my spirit guide, and she answered, "It's just the way it is."

There may be incidents in our lives—a close call in a car or plane, or perhaps difficulty waking from an anesthetic after surgery, for example, when we have a choice to exit. We have no choice when the fifth exit point arrives, though. Sometimes that final exit point can be elongated ten years on either side. Still, any way you look at it, death is a certainty for all of us. The ones left behind are metaphorically still in class until their "graduation" to the Other Side.

The comforting thing is that we will all perfect our destiny, even if we go through it kicking and screaming. We choose our own course of study. It's during those hard and painful experiences that we learn the most and strengthen our souls. Eventually we are able to feel relief from the grief, but not from the loss. The more spiritually advanced we become, the more our perception widens, and there's a greater scope of awareness. This also means that you feel pain to a greater degree.

As you advance spiritually throughout your lifetimes, the lessons become harder. When this happens and we agree to take on the harder tests, one of the most difficult "courses" is grief. This is the ultimate stage of learning. Those who have not lived many lives are not going to take on a lot of pain or responsibility. We who are experiencing and living in the grief process decided to take on the most difficult course and learn the hardest of lessons in the School of Life. There is no doubt that by experiencing grief, you will advance spiritually. Nothing is ever gained spiritually without gut-level work.

Realizations

Some days are better than others. Sometimes when I have a good day, I almost feel guilty that I'm not sad. I'm grateful that I've been shown, through your inspiration and my own exploration of my feelings that remembering you doesn't always have to bring sadness.

When I thought of you today, my heart was filled with joy. I want you to know that I am a much better person for having had you in my life. I still want to share my life with you, and I want your continued infusion of inspiration and knowledge.

Notes for Reflection

Nancy's Thoughts

I've found that as I continue to progress on my journey, more and more is revealed to me. In fact, I find answers to questions in the strangest places. I seem to get communications from my father while I'm just walking around doing my grocery shopping or driving in the car. Interestingly enough, now that I think about it, after Mom died, Daddy and I spent a lot of time in the car running errands, and we would go grocery shopping once or twice a week together. It seemed to be where we did most of our talking.

My father has always given me very specific communications. He actually led me to find something that was his mother's that I was looking for in his house. Daddy has also directed me to some Bible quotations to find answers to my requests for help. Never once in his life did my father quote the Bible to me, so that one's out of character, but it reminds me to keep my mind open and not discount anything. Sometimes Daddy gives me answers in a song or in puzzle form. He leaves it for me to discover their meaning, which again, as I think of it, is so like him.

My dad was always clear on exactly what he wanted to say; he didn't mince words much. He also considered it his fatherly duty to make me think for myself so I could take care of myself. On the other hand, my mother seems to just infuse her voice and knowledge right into my head. Mothers tend to make things easier for their children.

So listen and look everywhere. People who love you never leave you; they're there to help you on this journey.

Realization

Through our continued spiritual relationship, I will find a way past the walls around me. The vine of love will continue to grow and bloom. It may grow over or under the wall; it may even grow through a tiny space barely visible, but certainly it will seek the light for nourishment and life. So, too, will I seek the light for nourishment and enlightenment.

Notes for Reflection

Sylvia's Thoughts

Pain is relative for all of us. I've heard of people trying to top each other as far as who's had the worst surgery, the most difficult childbirth, the most lost loves, and so on. This is all useless when it comes to your own individual pain. However, we can tell you about *ours*, which will hopefully be a catharsis for you so that you'll know you're not alone.

All else aside, it will be *your* personal journey to ride that dark horse into those caverns of despair. I've actually seen my loved ones who have passed to the Other Side. I've even briefly talked to them. Still, even I, a clairvoyant and clairaudient, cannot just call them up or make a date for lunch.

Grief is actually selfish. We want that person we lost for ourselves. We want to see, touch, hear, and be with them. There is no easy way to go through grief. The pain ebbs and peaks, and there's no time limit on this pain. It has a razor's edge.

There's no way to put a pain threshold on our losses, and attached to the grief, there's anger. Most of the time we don't see the sense in our losses. The loss of a child is especially devastating because it's not the "right" order of things. We also don't care who's lost their child, spouse, or parent—we just know we did not want to lose ours!

People may say, "Look at all the other people who have lost loved ones. . . ." We just don't care! We didn't want it to be someone *we* loved. Society places guilt on us for having these feelings. People say, "You *must* just go on with your life!"

Well, going on with your life may simply be going on with your grieving process, because *that's* a part of your life. You'll get sick if you don't grieve. You must allow yourself that indulgence. As I said before, there's no time limit! A part of it always stays with us, as does the love for the person we've lost.

When grieving, we truly experience unconditional love. We tend to remember the good times, positive qualities, and precious memories, rather than the dark days or arguments that took place. In time, we learn to deal with our grief and cope with it—but we never forget.

All of a sudden, one day, you'll get to the point when you notice that you had ten minutes or a half hour when your mind wasn't obsessed with loss and felt some semblance of peace. Then you may worry that you'll forget the details of that person or the love you felt, but you won't—it will always be a part of your life; it just begins to change character and form. The cord between you and the person you love never breaks, but you learn to let the slack out a little bit, and the sharp edge of pain softens to a duller edge.

Sometimes we're overpowered by a deep depression. This type of depression is a hole in the ground with no light to be found. We may wake up feeling that there's nothing to live for, and by noon we're sure of it! Just keep in mind that this situational depression is nothing to be ashamed of, and it's part of the process for many.

In grief, there is a tremendous need to ventilate and ease our pain. The need helps us seek out ways of moving through the confusion and shock accompanying the death of a loved one. It helps us to understand how life will go on, and know with certainty that it *does* go on.

In time, precious time, you will see that there's nothing to life but what we make of it. As the sharpness of the pain dulls and the situational depression lifts, clarity will replace much of the haze and conflicting emotions.

You may wonder why we create these attachments and feel so permanent about this life and the people in it. If we didn't form these family ties, deep loves, friendships, and feelings of closeness, we wouldn't stay. We need to realize that we're only trying to find a way of getting through this time of grief and longing until we're with those we love again—and we surely will be.

If you just relax in your grief, you'll see evidence that your loved ones are still *with* you and *around* you. You'll find it in your dreams; you'll also notice things intuitively and feel a sense of their presence.

Realization

Through my writings, I have endless ways to continue a relationship with my loved ones. I use this avenue to open myself up to hearing and seeing in a new way. I can now live with hope rather than despair. I can be with, instead of without.

Notes for Reflection

_____

_____

_____

_____

_____

_____

_____

_____

_____

_____

_____

Nancy's Thoughts

This may sound odd, but it's true.

I've had a fear of death since I was about four years old. My mother used to sit with me in the middle of the night when I would wake up begging her to call a priest or the Pope or someone to see if I could be exempted from this fate. This went on all throughout my childhood. In my adult life, I would just lie silently with the same fears of death, but never speak of it. I feared that death would mean being isolated, being separated from loved ones, or worst of all, being punished for the human errors I made during my life. Still, I think that my biggest fear was existing in nothingness, isolated forever and ever, waiting for an occasional visit from a saint or God, which made me gasp for breath. It still makes me a little queasy thinking about it. I was taught about heaven, but it never really sounded like it was a place that I wanted to spend eternity in. I decided I'd rather stay here on Earth where I was sure of what was going on.

Sylvia will attest to my fears, as I've also shared them with her. Even with all the validations I've gotten on my own and through *her* views on life after death, it didn't completely erase the old tapes in my head. I wanted more proof!

When my mother died, I felt her presence continually for more than five months. I wanted to see her, yet I was partially afraid to and partially angry that I didn't. I felt her as I moved through my day. I could sense her being physically next to me, and her presence filled our house. There was a thickness, not unlike the sensation I felt around me at the time of her death. I felt warm spots and cool spots for no logical reason.

I began to realize that she was still mothering me because she felt my pain, as she did in life. She was watching over my infant son and my husband, while I muddled through my grief. She was with us, no question about it. There was that wrapped-in cotton feeling around me most of the time. Yet, to a degree, I still feared death.

I felt that Mom came to me to help me know that I had my own life plan to work out. She had come to mother me a little bit more because I was in such desperate need of her attention. My world was spinning out of control, and my mom was here to teach me to slow it down so I could find my own way.

My husband confirmed my feelings of Mom's presence, and even mentioned that he saw her next to me in the kitchen. Sometimes he'd see her sitting with me on the bed as I would feed our son or read a book. I told him that I had asked Mom to prove to me that there was life after death so I would never be afraid again.

I was a bit upset that I couldn't see *her*, too. It took me months to realize that she was, in fact, proving what I asked. She did it through her presence and by sharing her visual self with Paul. She needed to prove it slowly, for she knew that if I saw her sitting next to me, I might fall over and faint. Even in life, she used to talk to Paul and ask him to do certain things to take care of me and protect me, and she was just continuing in that familiar pattern.

I started to accept and believe more and more in what I was feeling and sensing around me. I actually grew to love the feeling of her presence, and I became attached to it like a baby with a blanket. It's all about taking that deep breath and relaxing in your grief, as Sylvia says, for when you do, then you find the validations, communications, and visitations.

When Mom was alive, we probably talked to each other a minimum of four to five times a day. So when Mom was buried, I symbolically put a portable phone in her coffin, complete with speed-dial numbers that went directly to me.

About three months after her death, I was just longing to see her and hear her voice. One early morning, about 2 A.M., the phone rang and I got up and walked into the kitchen to answer it. I remember feeling foggy and dream-like. I sat in the chair by the phone and clearly heard my mother's voice. It felt comforting and familiar, and I felt so at ease. While I heard her voice, I actually did see her in my peripheral vision, moving closer and closer to me very slowly. In fact, I saw her in vivid color. Mom's hair was a soft brown with auburn highlights, and her olive skin looked as smooth as silk. I remember how pink her cheeks and lips were. Her eyes were clear and chocolate brown, and I could see memories we had together by just looking into her eyes. It was as if she was showing me home movies that signified specific times in our life together.

What was so pleasing and such a relief to me was that she looked vibrant, absolutely beautiful, and quite young and healthy. For all the suffering she had done and how her illness had stolen her essence, I could see that she had it all again—and more. In life, I never saw her look so content and peaceful.

The details of her dress were astounding. She was wearing a mid-length dress with three layers of flowing white, very pale peach material that had hints of an ecru color running through it, and it seemed to radiate light. I also recall a pale blue shawl draped loosely over one shoulder. At the same time, I could hear her voice on the phone, but when I looked at her, I didn't see her mouth moving; she just smiled gently and pleasantly.

I have no idea how long I sat there in that chair with the phone in my hand, but I know that I *did* drop the receiver from my ear and was holding it in my lap. Nevertheless, I could still hear her, and she could still hear me. I remember asking her questions nonverbally, and she answered me telepathically. It was as clear as day.

When I finally started to replace the receiver, I recall that there was no sound on the phone, not even the sound that it makes when you've left it off the hook too long. As I stood up, the image of Mom backed away from me as carefully as it appeared. I memorized what I had seen—her face, her dress, her look—everything—for in some way I knew that this clear vision probably would not come again.

I remember physically walking back to the bedroom, pulling the covers back and getting back into bed. As I was doing so, I stirred Paul a little, and he asked me who was on the phone. I told him that it was my mom, but we never really spoke of it much; we both just went to sleep. I don't recall looking at the clock to see how long I was out of bed, but it seemed like quite a long time—maybe hours, I don't know.

The next day, I really felt as if I had spent hours with my mother, as if we'd had a long soulful visit and caught up on the time we had missed together. I also recalled that what she had said to me was not just about catching up, but about the future, and her reassuring me that she was always with me and that we would be together again some-day. I felt like she was easing my fears of death in a way that she could not do for me while she was alive. It was so like her to not give up trying to help me.

For the first time in my life, I didn't try to logically explain away the occurrence of the night before. My heart felt full. I knew that my mother had been with me on a level that was incredible, and it filled me with love.

I wasn't sure exactly how this was happening, though. Was Mom communicating with me in a dream, or was it an actual visitation? I have never been quite sure. It felt dreamlike; however, I was physically up and out of my bed and in the kitchen holding the phone and sitting in the chair. Have I ever been prone to sleepwalking? Never once, so this event remains something of a mystery, yet it was clearly a communication with my mother.

Ultimately, it didn't matter how it happened. The fact is that it *did* happen, and my mother loved me so much that she transcended whatever barriers there might have been for her so that she could be with me one more time. The feeling of having my mother so near, and the sound of her voice, was unmistakable.

This was the only time that I have seen and felt this

degree of intense communication with my mother, and it has become one of my most treasured memories. I would like it to happen again, and although I don't expect it to, I remain open to it.

Mom's strong presence continued for about two more months, and then one day, it just felt like she had moved on. I said to Paul, "I think Mom is gone."

He replied, "She is. The house is clear now."

I now feel her specific presence from time to time, but it feels more as if she's just checking in on us and reminding me that there really is more. Now, I always listen carefully to the intuitive feelings that come to me—even those that do not make immediate sense or that seem to fly into my head for no particular reason. No matter how minor or major the feeling or thought, I never ignore my inner voice.

There were a couple of times that I didn't listen and just pushed the feeling aside. It became immediately clear that I neither trusted myself, nor the messages and guidance I was being privileged to receive. But now I'm convinced that these intuitive feelings or premonitions come from a loving source.

I continue to write to my mother through letters in my journal, asking her for assistance, knowledge, and guidance. I still hear her voice regularly, although it's hard to explain how. It's as if I hear her communicating to me nonverbally, yet her words *are* audible in a sense. And I *do* get answers.

I sense Mom's comforting demeanor, yet I still ache for her tangible physical touch. The experience I had with her does give me a sense of peace, yet I'm not exempt from the days when all of a sudden my tears and panic replace the knowledge that she's still with me, as well as the realization that we will all be together again someday.

I've let some of the slack out on the cord, but it's still a strong cord—one that will never be broken. The pain is still more sharp than dull, but I do have moments of peace that I no longer feel guilty for, and the moments of memories and closeness of spirit I have with my mother are a welcome relief from the emptiness.

I try to give my emotions the same understanding I give my body. A cut or incision does not heal the moment it is inflicted, but it does *start* to heal. The injury may leave a scar or be tender to the touch forever, but the wound surely does close up. It will heal to the degree that one is reminded of the injury, but it is no longer open and raw.

I now know that the love that I felt in life with my parents is still felt in their absence. It may feel nonreciprocal at first, but it's not.

In time, you feel a person's love from the Other Side encompassing you in both familiar and new ways. It surrounds you and gives you dimension and fullness. You just need to learn to feel it and recognize the ways in which it may be new to you. The pain of grief is the path to learning, and it *does* give birth to heightened spiritual awareness and perfection.

There is growth through suffering, and for me, the process continues.

Realization

If we deny our grief, we deny living. If we look at memories and find them painful, we should look closer. We may find that the memory is one of joy, and the pain only comes from missing those times.

Notes for Reflection

_____

_____

_____

_____

_____

_____

_____

_____

_____

_____

_____

_____

_____

_____

_____

_____

_____

_____

_____

_____

_____

_____

Sylvia's Thoughts

Nancy's fear of death is, of course, something I've always known about. Nancy has shared it with me and has struggled with it for years. I think what she fears more than death is the fear of nothingness—that she and all those she loves will cease to be.

Little by little, I have watched this dear girl come along step by step on her own spiritual path. I could not help her in the way I wanted to, but no one can, because it is each person's individual course. The loss of Nancy's parents intensified her fear and increased the pain.

I wanted to take her pain away, as I know she wanted to take away mine, but we could not do that for each other. So in our own way, we fought through the hell alone, but still side by side. Neither of us ever forgot the loss or stopped missing the physical presence of our loved ones, or stopped grieving for them.

We did slowly and certainly find healing, though—a little more each day. I'm proud of Nancy for not being paralyzed by her fears. I'm proud of her for facing her fears while moving forward. I'm also proud of us for fighting side by side and being each other's champion when the other did not have the strength in the moment. That connection with another soul is also part of one's spiritual journey and perfection.

There are many people who struggle with fears of death and of ceasing to exist. The death of a loved one brings those fears to the forefront. To those of you who identify, continue this journey with us and you, too, will find your way, little by little, on your own spiritual path. You will come to know that there is more than this Earthly life.

Exercise

Just before you go to sleep, ask that the white light of the Holy Spirit surround you. Ask for angels to stand by your bed. Begin to visualize a dark velvet sky, and feel the peace of this softness enveloping you. All of a sudden, you see a pinpoint of light piercing through, and it seems to be coming toward you. Then ask for your loved ones to come toward you in that light. Don't even think or use the word *imagination*. It is the one word that has ruined psychic ability and visions, and has even inhibited getting closer to God.

Your loved ones may first appear in silhouette, but eventually you will see them.

Realizations

Be kind to yourself. Don't push yourself. Know that this is one of the most difficult challenges that you will ever go through, and go through it you must. Be gentle and tolerant of yourself. Always keep in mind that when facing the dragon of grief, you are given the opportunity to go through the greatest spiritual journey that you will ever travel.

When I feel pity for myself, I treat myself as a friend. I treat myself with patience and acceptance. I don't judge what I'm feeling. I don't judge my friends, so why judge myself? Enough other people do the judging for you.

Notes for Reflection

Nancy's Thoughts

As I've progressed through the deaths of my grandparents, my aunt and uncle whom I loved deeply, many friends, and most devastating of all, both of my parents, I've had to face the fears that I tried so hard to put away under lock and key. I have tried every way I know of to run from the pain, but it lives inside of me, so there's really nowhere to run.

There is really only one choice or option—to learn to coexist with my grief. I must acknowledge the sadness that overcomes me from time to time as part of being human, and admit that sometimes I may need to lean on another human being to move forward through those sad times. Sometimes I may need to ask for spiritual strength and direction. Basically, I must know that to ask for help is not a weakness, but a wise choice.

I've been given many validations, both personally and through things that Sylvia has shared with me. I have no doubt that my parents and other family and friends continue to exist, and I never go a day without feeling Mom or Daddy close to me. Oftentimes I feel one or more of my grandparents near. It's hard to explain how. It's a thought, a smell, a feeling, a song, something someone says, or a situation that is too exact to be a coincidence.

When my mother died, I was privileged to be a part of her transition Home. I was a part of something so much greater than I could have ever imagined or been told. In her death, I felt so lost and yet so certain that I would surely see her again. That gave me a shred of sanity that I have held tightly to ever since. It helped me to remember that feeling when I lost Daddy. I had hoped to be with him when he died—both for him and also for me. I wanted to be a part of whatever it was that surrounded my mother and me when she went Home. I wanted to feel that certainty again. However, I'm grateful for feeling and knowing that sensation at least once; it helps me to move ahead in my journey.

I still have spiritual work to do and faith to deepen, and I believe that this process will be ongoing. I think that my old fears will creep into my thoughts and try to pull me backwards, but now I know that my momentum will primarily be a forward movement, with the help of my parents and grandparents who still keep me close. Finding your way is individual, yet it's never done completely alone. I constantly ask my parents to help me or to remind me that they're with me, and I get their help in many different ways. I never stop communicating with them. To stop would be like ignoring them when they were alive. They're not here on this Earth, but they're just in another place, and our communications have taken on new and deeper forms.

Do I still fear death? Sometimes, but now my fear is that I don't want to leave anyone that I love here, especially my husband and son. I want to be here for my child as long as possible, but when I can't, I hope he will pick up his mama's and grandma's journal and know that we are right there with him, continuing to love him and help him through his journey. I hope my precious son will know as I am continuing to learn and know . . . that love never dies.

Realization

Love is the strong connection that keeps us in touch with those on the Other Side—even through different dimensions. It is the love we have shared that allows our friends and relatives to continue to be with us until we are ultimately together again.

Notes for Reflection

_____

_____

_____

_____

_____

_____

_____

_____

_____

_____

_____

_____

_____

_____

_____

_____

_____

_____

_____

Sylvia's Thoughts

Recently I was on the phone talking to a client who had lost her sister, and every night the sister would come to her and sit on her bed and have long talks with her.

I almost hit the proverbial ceiling.

In the kindest way possible, I began to explain to this woman that her sister was so real because she hadn't made it through the tunnel from this dense vibration to the Other Side, where vibration goes at a higher rate of speed.

Besides, if entities are coming around too often, that means that they're Earthbound and have not made the transition.

Even though the person who is still on this side may *want* those long talks and chances to say things that were never said, it's not fair to hold spirits here on this plane. When this happens, you need to direct the spirits toward the light and release them so they can find their way Home to the Other Side.

I know what you're thinking—the same thing that the human part of me almost got caught up in: "If only I could have had one last talk with my son, daughter, husband, sister, wife, parent," and so on.

Think about it, though: How many last talks could we have, and really, would that give us closure? No! We get a sense of finality on the part of our life that is gone, but there is never total closure in this life. It isn't meant to be. It is our charted journey, and when that time is over, we leave or we are left. Death is truly the graduation of our time on Earth, the classroom of learning for God, and when we've learned all that we have charted to learn, we graduate.

I constantly hear, "Why did they have to go now? Things were just beginning to get better. Why did they go so young? They had their whole life ahead of them." Well, even as I passed through my own grief, I recognized that we have just so many hours, months, days, and years to spend here, and when that time is over, we go.

The other thing we hear people say is, "Only the good die young." That's ridiculous. If that were true, then shall we assume that all the elderly folks of this world are bad people? Of course they aren't.

The other comment I've heard is: "God wanted them to come Home." Remember that God does not play favorites.

I've also heard people say something similar to, "I must be going through this terrible time because I'm paying for something I did." Why would someone else die so you could pay, and most important, God is *not* vengeful.

If we could just stop thinking that life is all there is, we would be much happier. We are, of course, supposed to have strong survival instincts, and if we all really remembered, we wouldn't stay here. We can't break the contract by taking our own life because then we just have to come back to this hell (yes, *this* is where it is) and do the same things again, only more intensely.

If Jesus could go to Gethsemane and ask God to remove the painful chalice from him and he got a "no," what chance do *we* have? Does that mean that God is uncaring? No, just the opposite. God knows that we choose our own chart, but when we get down here, like a child in the wilderness, we want to cancel the whole deal.

God, all-knowing and merciful, is trying to keep us from making the same mistakes and glorify our souls to reach an even higher level of joy when we cross over.

Parents cannot be effective if they let their kids renege on the contracts they've agreed upon. We come down fresh from the Other Side full of bliss and peace, and then the lessons we've chosen begin, and we scream, "I didn't know it was going to be this hard. I want out!" Instead of seeing this as a cruel, predestined trial of pain and doom, why not take a reality check. If the subjects were easy and everything was perfect, why come here?

You come here, as I stated previously, to expand your soul, and as your soul expands through pain and grief, it also expands in knowing and loving and moving toward a state of bliss. When you resonate to this truth, you will find a light at the end of this grief tunnel. The light is filled with echoes, memories, and a kaleidoscope of what was and what will never be—although it *will be* on the Other Side. The finality is only here. Our lives are a tiny drop in an ocean of infinity.

We've had lives when we've been used; and when we've felt alone, rejected, and have experienced loss, and so on—the list is endless. The one common denominator is the grief we've felt. Every soul, unless it is empty and dark, resonates to grief, strangely even more than it does to love.

Love is the tie that binds us to each other and to God, but grief binds us stronger here because it is the one primary lesson that is relegated to this planet. Love is forever, and grief is transient. No one on the Other Side grieves. Even if you're going to live to be 100, to those on the Other Side, you'll be there with them in a few days. You're talking about us being timebound and trying to reference a place (the Other Side) where there is no time boundary.

In my early days of going into trance, a woman who had recently lost her husband asked Francine, my spirit guide, what she was going to do without him. Francine told her, "It doesn't matter. You will be with him in a few weeks . . ." Well, when I came out of trance, this poor woman was over in the corner talking about getting her affairs in order, and she was just frantic.

I asked her what had happened, as I don't remember what Francine says when I'm in trance, and the woman said, "I only have a few weeks to live!"

I thought, *How horrible!* But I wondered about it and went into my office and asked Francine to explain. Francine told me that the woman had about 30 years left, according to *our* time. I asked her why she told her she only had a few weeks, and Francine replied, "That's about all it amounts to over here."

So I went out and explained to the woman that Francine was referencing another time frame in another dimension.

Do those on the Other Side care if you don't visit their grave sites? No, they're not there. Do they care what you do with their Earthly possessions? No, they're not going to use things. Do they care if you had a fight right before they passed? No, because they have the whole plan in front of them now. Do they care if you didn't get a chance to say good-bye? No, and if you feel bad, say it now. They'll hear you. All the "I should have done and didn't do" things (and I could go on forever) are wasted. They are part of our own self-ordained guilt processes, and yes, even our selfishness—mine and yours.

What if a person has numerous husbands or wives or many siblings? Will they all get along on the Other Side? No one can fool the soul. The soul knows who the kindred souls are and who the one soulmate is, so there's no jealousy or envy or disharmony.

Another thing: Francine tells me that personalities don't melt over there. We aren't all walking around with carbon copy looks, characteristics, or personalities. That's a relief. However, groups with the same affinity do stay together. We don't just cling to our soulmate alone, though; we have other souls in our group. Sometimes soulmates do not always choose to be together.

There is debate and discussion on the Other Side, but not anger or grudges. It is similar to the way it is here, only we're always healthy and happy. Eventually we all lose each other, but be assured that we find each other again on the Other Side.

Those on the Other Side are sublimely happy and are also reassured to know that you will go through your tests, just as they did, and pass whether you like it or not, finally joining them at Home. The Home we came from and were created from and lived in before we came here into this life is the same Home we will eventually go back to and live forever in with our loved ones.

It's almost like a parent getting a letter from a child who's at camp who writes that he's homesick and begs to come home. The parent knows that the experience is good for the child and that he will eventually adjust. Then at the end of the session, Mom and Dad will drive to the camp and pick the child up and tell him how proud they are because he stuck it out. The child, sitting there beside his parents, looks back and sees that it wasn't so bad after all, and that there were some good memories. And he also feels pride, resonating from the knowledge that "I'm really stronger than I thought, and I did make it! Maybe, just maybe, I'll go again next year to see if I can be even stronger."

So lives go on, one after another, until we've conquered

a lot of our fears, abandonment issues, and more. Then the soul grows in *true* pride, not false pride. This goes on until we don't need to go to camp anymore. And then we can stay at Home.

Whether you're aware of it or not, we all suffer from Homesickness here. We're separated not only from loved ones, but we also miss not having any cares and worries. We long for a state of loving that knows no ego and hostility. Here, we are flawed, and weighted down with a body that functions the best it can, but it is laborious at best. We have the stress of families, jobs, finances, loss, loneliness, and more.

But if we live with the knowledge that this is all ephemeral, and if we let God in and let go, trust me, it makes life glide along rather than jerk along.

So, don't *fight* the current; go with it. Does it hurt? Yes, something awful, but it passes. Do you forget? Never. Does time heal? Not totally. You learn to survive it, but it is always a wound that can break open at any given time and bleed again.

No one can stay on that razor's edge. We would die from that intensity, and there are often times when we wish for death. But the world crowds in, and we have other loved ones in our lives, so we keep our little altars in our hearts.

There is also a type of grief that results from broken relationships. Being abandoned is just as real and many times even more devastating than death. At least death is natural, but an abandoned love is crushing and is the ultimate rejection.

So this journey is for all of us who have losses related to life or death. We are kindred spirits under the burden of this human body. We have loved and we have lost, and we are feeling alone.

Remember, though: You may *feel* alone, but truly you are not. Those who have gone are with us. God is with us, and our angels are with us, and we are with each other.

Let out your torment in these pages, even your guilt and your longings. Express your rage at what might have been. I bet if you're faithful in writing down your feelings, as time goes on, you'll read your own words when you're further along in your journey, and you'll be so very proud of how far you've come.

Realization

Mourning is a constant reflection and adjustment. It is the ever-present knowledge that I must find ways to live with my loss, and not let my loss live in place of me.

Notes for Reflection

_____

_____

_____

_____

_____

_____

_____

Nancy's Thoughts

In the initial days after my mother's death, I felt as if I were on a roller coaster. I was numb, then physically ill, and yet somehow I was able to go through the motions and take on my daily responsibilities. I was definitely mentally weak and unable to complete a thought, yet the paradox was that I *was* able to make the mundane decisions that needed to be made in my daily life. It was as if my mind went on automatic pilot part of the time, and my intellect overrode my emotional state. I was like a yo-yo. If it had not been for my then four-month-old son, I might have been consumed by the emptiness in my heart.

There have been moments when I never thought I would get to a point where I could be proud of my pain and grief. Now, however, I'm so sure that this is a noble, life-altering journey that I'm finally able to share it with those of you whom I may have never met, but surely know heart-to-heart and through our common bond.

When my mother, who was an integral part of my daily life, died, I felt that she had abandoned me and left me in a world I just couldn't face. I believed that her absence from my life and from my son's future was the most brutal pain I would ever know. I fought that pain by going into a type of withdrawal and by ignoring the steps I would have to eventually take in order to heal. I threw myself into mothering my son (my angel), but all others I kept at arm's distance for a while—even, Paul, the love of my life. I did this in case I lost him, too. Then there was Daddy, whose pain over the loss of his mother and wife in the same week was devastating to his strong nature. He hid it fairly well, but it came out in various ways. Watching him grieve was shaking my own attempt to ignore my feelings.

Finally, one morning as I was dusting Mom's dresser, Daddy, in a panic, said, "Don't put her perfume bottle so far back; she always kept it more forward." I sat on the floor and looked up at his face and saw someone I had never seen before.

He was so lost and full of what looked like a child's fear. He had worked so hard to hide it from me, but it had become too much now. I just melted like an ice cube in the sun. I lost all of my composure and sobbed like a little girl. For a moment, my father and I were children together—age knew no boundaries. Daddy reached out his hand and said, "I'm not your mother, but I *am* your father, and I'm here and I love you." As I took his hand, our relationship forever changed.

Mom was always the softhearted one, the one we ran to, to plead our case with Daddy. She was our ally and champion and always our friend. Daddy believed in structure, thinking that each day offered us a lesson in life and an opportunity to learn something we could keep for the future. Daddy made the rules, and Mom helped us bend them. Daddy was always strong, and he kept his promise— good or bad. He was my father—a man who protected me and whom I trusted—a man who kept his vulnerability carefully guarded for so many years.

Even the night that I had to go to his house and tell him that Mom had just died, his eyes spoke to the depth of his pain, but he remained calm and strong in my presence. But on this day, he revealed the person he had so often kept hidden. He again saved me from my own self-destruction by showing me that we all need someone to help us find our way and the truth of our journey, and that this is not a weakness.

From that day forward, Daddy and I became friends. He and I grew to depend on and love one another, more each day. We continued to buck heads and banter, yet we always worked through our differences, for we knew we were all that was left of what we once had. He would tell me stories about my mother that I loved to hear, and I would share things about Mom that he hadn't known. We became the bridge and link to her, as well as each other's lifeline to the family we had once been a part of. We even laughed as we shared memories.

Sometimes Daddy would look at me and say, "I see your mother in you." And he'd smile when my eyes filled with tears, for there were times when I would look in the mirror and see it, too, and it would take me by surprise and make me happy. He told me he loved me more in those few years after Mom's passing than he ever had in my whole life. So, a lot of good did come from my mother's passage Home to God.

Now, I truly thought that after losing Mom, I was prepared for anything. I am here to say that the second blow of grief almost devastated me completely. One loss does not prepare you for another. I felt crippled in the aftermath of Daddy's death. By the time he died, I had lost all my grandparents, my aunt and uncle, many close family friends, and my mother.

The moment that Daddy died, the walls went up. I immediately decided to insulate myself from loving another human being too much. I felt that if I did not step back from all relationships, I would surely be destroyed. I pushed my husband away, leaving him helpless and confused, and I withdrew from friends and what was left of my family. Again, though, my darling angel son was my source of reality and love. I could not push him away. He was the reason my heart was still beating. We needed each other, for now he understood loss. He grieved for his Nonno (grandfather) and needed understanding, guidance, and comfort. The only time I felt whole was when I was with my son.

That doesn't mean I didn't let him see me cry; it simply means that I was able to meet his needs and honestly talk with him about what was happening. Interestingly, though, many times my little son comforted and reassured *me*. He would tell me that Nonno was not feeling sadness now, and would say that he could see him dancing in the clouds with Nonnie (grandmother). He told me that Nonno was feeling good, could breathe easily, and was smiling. He told me that my daddy did not want me to be sad.

Children are amazing gifts, and they center us and keep us focused, showing us what is really important.

Keeping my son close to my heart was all I wanted and seemed able to do; everything else was too much for me. During this time, I was literally terrified. I did not want to leave the house, talk on the phone, eat, or sleep. I lived in a world that was like nothing I had ever experienced. My world became surrealistic and unfamiliar. I *did* find myself going to my parents' home, however. I sat at my dad's desk wearing a shirt of his; it smelled like his soap on a rope. I slept in his pajamas and hugged his pillow, finding comfort in surrounding my senses with his smell. I still do that at times. I can even remember one time just coming unglued when my husband put Daddy's pillow under his head. I jumped up frantically and said, "Don't use that, it's Daddy's; don't put your smell on it." My husband actually understood my point, even though my method was a bit "out there." I was an orphan—I knew it, and my husband knew it.

I found that I kept going to my parents' house. I was searching for a piece of them that I could hold on to. But the reality was, I was on my own, left on this Earth without them. The thought still makes me shiver and brings tears streaming down my face.

Through the loss of my parents, I came dangerously close to letting go of everyone I loved deeply. I rationalized that I might as well start letting go now, and feel the numbing pain, for surely they would all leave me eventually, some time, in some way. It was as close to going over the edge into darkness as I have ever known. I was struggling on a daily basis—mentally, emotionally, and physically. My grief began to take on real physical manifestation.

The panic attacks started almost immediately after Daddy died. I could not catch my breath, I became overwhelmed with tremors, and my legs couldn't hold me up. My heart felt as if it was about to explode, and my head was so thick with a foglike feeling that I'm lucky I had speed dial so I could call for help. I knew that I could call Sylvia and her husband, Larry.

Sylvia knew firsthand how emotional pain affected the body. She and Larry would literally talk me out of being paralyzed from panic and loneliness. Sometimes it took minutes, and other times, an hour. The attacks usually hit at night, and I didn't have a second's warning. This is not the type of information one usually shares with just anyone. I feel no shame for having had this physical reaction, though. Admitting this now gives me courage and purpose.

There are still times when I get revisited by one of these unmistakable attacks, but I understand that they are a reaction to the despair and pain that jumps up and slaps me across the face from time to time.

I am still on this excruciating journey, but now I'm able to love and be loved again, and that's the difference between taking this journey in the light with other kindred souls, or in the darkness, alone, with unshared pain and fears that torture your every moment.

There are gifts given to each of us through loss. My gifts have been many more than I would have thought at the time. I have been given the knowledge that I will be reunited with those I love someday. I am able to look at my husband and feel grateful for who he is, and treasure that he is still here, loving me throughout all my nightmares and my out-of-control episodes. I am able to accept friendship, and cherish and nurture it in a way that I could not before my world shattered. I have no doubt about what is important and what is petty. I know what's worth standing up for and what's not worth the waste of energy to argue about. I am definitely stronger for all of my weakness and vulnerability. I have become a better parent, wife, and friend overall—with the ability to truly treasure the important things in life.

My relationship with Sylvia has been so enhanced and deepened—on both sides. We have been able to travel hand-in-hand through the dragon's den, and we can cry for each other with unconditional love and understanding. Through this journey together, we're able to offer others what we've found in each other—a mirrored soul to walk each painful step from the darkness into the light. I treasure the look in Sylvia's eyes, the feel of her warm touch, and her strong and understanding arms around me. I'm deeply grateful that I have a place to go to be a child again and find love and guidance.

This ache for belonging and nurturing happens to all parentless children, no matter what the age. It also happens to widows and widowers. We all *need* other human beings. That's why it's so vital that we not isolate ourselves in our grief, for doing so will certainly wither our spirits. The purpose of grief is to expand us spiritually and allow us opportunities to give to those who share the same treacherous course.

Giving back is equally important. What I value as much as receiving support is being given the privilege to be there for Sylvia. Offering her the priceless comfort she always gives me helps us both grow and progress. Letting her be a child in my arms brings a sense of trust and contentment to both of us and gives me a feeling of being honored by her.

Who we are and who we are becoming is defined by what we have experienced. This personal, yet universal, journey is a metamorphosis in progress. We must help each other.

Realization

My umbilical cord to those I miss and continue to love is woven and protected through my words on these precious pages. I am able to write my thoughts and feelings about my daily life, and also ask for help and guidance through letters to my loved ones. I listen carefully for their responses.

Notes for Reflection

_____

_____

_____

_____

_____

_____

_____

_____

_____

_____

_____

_____

_____

_____

_____

_____

_____

Sylvia's Thoughts

When I was 15 years old, I fell in love for the first time with a boy named Warren. He lived in Kansas City, Missouri, where I went to a Catholic high school. We dated for about a year, but our biggest problem had to do with the differences in our belief systems. At that time, Warren didn't even know if God existed.

I remember that on Easter morning after just attending church, I went into one of my long diatribes, and I said, "Warren, all things come from God." At that very moment, a bird decided to relieve himself in my open hand. He looked at me and said, "Point well taken."

Over the years, we would still get hysterical over that incident and would tell everyone the story. Anyway, I moved to California, and he did, too. I knew and loved his wife and the two boys they had. I taught school and did readings, and Warren was a lawyer. We would go for months and never talk, but we always knew we were there for each other. I would call him for his legal knowledge, and we would all go out to eat and have a catching-up visit. I became especially close to his wife, Pat; and to Michael, his youngest son. Warren never seemed quite happy—not because he didn't have a great career or a wonderful family, because he did. I always suspected that it was because his spirituality was buried. It was there, but it seemed that if he took it out, he'd have to act on it, and he was just too tired to do that. Was he a good man? Absolutely—very ethical and sensitive—but he couldn't show that very easily.

He eventually contracted cancer, I had told his wife that I saw his light fading about a year before. Sure enough, one year after he was diagnosed, he was dying. Dear Pat called me up and said he wouldn't see anyone else, but he *did* want to talk to me.

I went there with my heart in my mouth. This was another piece of me that no one would remember. Someone who remembered our childhood, our puppy love, and how life was then, was again leaving. We had grown up and gotten older with each other.

I sat down, and Warren said, "You know, I always acted like I never believed in all that foolishness you spouted, but Sylvia, tell me now."

I almost screamed, *You S.O.B., now that you're dying, you want to know what I've been trying to share with you all these years? We had so many years when we could have shared a truth, any truth, and now it's too late!* But then my intellect took over. *Why is it too late?* I asked myself. *It's perfect timing. When would he have listened before?*

We talked about the Other Side and how he would see the tunnel. He asked, "How do I get there?"

Then it hit me. It was so perfect. I knew he loved to fly; it was his passion. I said, "Warren, it's like when you're lifting off in your plane. You just taxi down the runway and pick up speed, and then you lift off. Just take three deep breaths, taxi, move faster, and take off."

He said, "Okay, sweetheart."

"I love you, Warren," I said.

He said, "I'll see you soon, Syl. Thanks for coming."

I was glad he had his eyes closed then, because my eyes were streaming with tears.

I kissed him and left the room. Then I kissed Pat and left them alone.

After I arrived home, Pat called and said, "Sylvia, Warren is gone. I was sitting with him and he just took three deep breaths and he was gone."

I said out loud, "Well, you old so-and-so, you *did* taxi and lift off."

❋ ❋ ❋

The pain of losing a lifelong friend, a foster child, and family members have all taken big chunks out of my essence. I know that a piece of me goes with them. But someday, I'll see you, Warren, Marvin, Curtis, Chris, Daddy, and Mama—and all those names too numerous to mention. We'll all sit under a tree in a meadow and tell jokes, remembering what was, and reminiscing about how glad we are to have made it through camp and are now together again.

In the meantime, I will hold Nancy close to me as my daughter, we will share our grief on dark nights, and we will cry without shame. We will try to live for our loved ones now, but we'll save the grief for the dark moments.

So, remember that you're not alone, not any of you. Each of you is tied together with us on this journey of spiritual development, emotional exploration, and discovery.

Let us join our hands to yours and say, "I know. I *really* know."

$\mathcal{E}$ x e r c i s e

Close your eyes and breathe deeply. Take yourself to a beautiful mountaintop. If you want to visualize climbing it, you can, or just relax and find yourself sitting on top of the mountain, overlooking the colorful, picturesque landscape— different shades of green and yellow on a sapphire sky.

Sit quietly while breathing in the sweet smell of spring flowers and freshly cut grass. Let the grief and the pain drain out from your body and mind. You're feeling great peace, knowing that your loved ones are standing behind you and beside you. It begins to rain, a soft gentle rain. With each drop, say, "God, please purge this pain and longing from my heart and replace it with the joy of having had this loved one in my life." Let your tears mingle with the rain, knowing that in the same way that your tears and the rain merge, so, too, will you will be merged with your loved ones on the Other Side.

Notes for Reflection

_____

_____

_____

_____

_____

_____

Nancy's Thoughts

Losing a person involves so much more than one single loss. It's an absence of the shared laughter or banter we've grown accustomed to. It's knowing that you can't run to this person for comfort or solace. It's also the absence of your being there for them. You not only miss what that person meant to you, but also what *you* were to the loved one who has gone Home. Your purpose seems to have shifted, and a piece of your daily life is missing. It seems like nothing will ever fit together in the same way again.

Loss creates the reality of having to live without this person who accepted you unconditionally. When you lose a partner, parent, child, or dear friend, it pushes you into a new way of life. It moves you forward on your journey, whether you're ready or not. At first it feels like it pushes you face down in the mud. But sometimes you need to just lie there and surrender to the fall before you find the strength to stand up on two legs and walk to the shower.

Being an adult can be unmerciful, and being responsible is so exhausting and draining. As long as you have your partner or parent, or that special sibling or friend, you're able to go somewhere to take a break and leave your adult responsibilities and logic behind, even for just a little while. We all need that break. We can run "home" to be a child for a precious few moments, and let the burden of adulthood lift, letting us remember the simple and silly things we love.

Once we go through the experience of having someone

we love pass over, that luxury we enjoyed with him or her seems lost. What actually happens is that eventually we do evolve and expand, and in doing so, we find that there's probably someone already in our life whom we can run to, to help us "quit" adulthood for a brief while.

We find these moments with others who know where we've been and are traveling the same path with us or ahead of us. These angels on Earth recognize themselves in us, for they are also longing for the lightheartedness of being a child again. So keep your eyes and your heart open; these wonderful individuals are all around—Sylvia being a prime example.

※ ※ ※

I have a dear friend who is now a young widow with two children. Her husband died suddenly. One day he was home for dinner, and the next day he was gone. All of a sudden, she had to be both mother and father, run a house, and now worry about repairs and car problems. From what she has shared, the hardest part of all was just getting out of bed to do all these other tasks. But she's also had to comfort the adults around her—who felt guilty about not being able to comfort *her*.

Again, it was the children who provided the clarity. As hard as it was to be both mother and father instantly, her children gave her the wings to find a way to help herself. She knew that she had to face her journey in order to hold her children's hands. so she sought out others who'd experienced the same type of loss.

She took the risk of opening her heart up to strangers, who, in turn, reached out and gently pulled her into a cocoon of love, knowledge, and understanding. They kept her safe there until she could fly a little way on her own, and eventually do the same for her children and others experiencing a similar loss.

From the moment she woke up and knew she was a widow, she's been challenged by life and its unpredictable twists and turns. What also never changes is the way in which she seeks out strength and knowledge and a road to spiritual progress. This has given her back what she thought was taken from her the moment her husband died.

I can see how some days are really hard for her, but because she's human, not superhuman, she's able to do a great job because she allows herself to be all that the word *human* implies, and that's inspirational to me. She never pretends that she has all the answers, but she usually has the means to find them. She never punishes herself for taking three steps back in a moment of loss revisited. She's learned the lesson in every step, be it forward or backward.

She and I learn from each other and teach each other daily. When the fog comes and surrounds our hearts, we know how to help each other. When decisions and responsibilities get to be too much, we know how to give each other a break and parent each other. I admire all of her strengths and her frailties, and I am so comforted by the fact that she's not made of forged steel, standing on a pedestal. She offers another place that's comfortable and real, and I can go there and be a silly, carefree child or a gloomy, lost little girl. I adore the fact that in all the seriousness we share, we can still be little girls revisiting some of the joy that we misplaced in our bottomless pit of grief.

In the same light, I have known and shared a welcome refuge with Sylvia. We have known side-bending laughter through the painful tears. Emotions are so often irrational and change like the wind. Still, if I laugh one minute and cry the next, Sylvia understands firsthand, because it makes perfect sense to her. That's a gift—to be able to let what you're feeling flow out no matter how it may appear, and to be with someone who doesn't think your behavior has no foundation. We're able to embrace and appreciate the times spent together, be it joyful and fun, or when the familiar flashes of pain grab us unexpectedly but surely. We expect that to happen, and we're learning to integrate it in our lives. We're able to share the best and worst of times with each other—no conditions and no questions. Actually, the losses in our lives have caused us to grasp each other tightly. Not only that, but we enjoy life much more than we would have had we never know the pain of bereavement, or had we never been a part of each other's pain. Shared pain offers comfort that isolated pain does not.

Looking back, I see now that I took so much for granted before I had the experience of heart-piercing loss. I just expected my parents to be there forever, I guess. I expected that I would always be someone's little girl, and I could always go home again to the place that held my childhood memories and my safety net. I imagined that I would have endless Christmas celebrations with them, and that they would be with me through every milestone in my son's life and in my own.

In the past, I would complain about little things that would ruin my day, such as a stain on the carpet or a broken crystal glass. Now I truly love life every day. Oh, I still get stressed out and worried, but I know what's important. I even recognize the gift in my sadness—the gift being that each day has endless miracles, and each person I love and who loves me is in my life for reasons constantly unfolding. I try to find at least one thing each day that makes that one different from all the rest—something positive. It really isn't hard to do. Even the days when I'm saturated in my feelings of grief, I'm able to be happy about something, even if it's just having loved people in my life so much that I now miss them terribly. Usually, though, life is an adventure, and each day is a lesson in how to handle it and appreciate what is positive and good.

Realization

Some people are uncomfortable with who I am becoming as a result of my loss. Some even feel fear. I see it in their faces. They don't know how to "act." If they only knew that "acting" is not what I need. If they only knew what gifts we could give each other through the experience of sorrow.

Notes for Reflection

_____

_____

_____

_____

Sylvia's Thoughts

How can speaking to the dead be evil or odd when so many people of various religions acknowledge that the soul survives death? In the old days, making us believe that this was wrong was a concerted effort to keep us under the thumb of dogma. Why was it that only the saints could have visions, but not us, and who determined who could be a saint?

Everyone who gets to heaven is a saint, and everyone who wants to go, gets there—even the ones who don't want to die and go Home to the Other Side.

Let's all address another seemingly tender issue here. This is not a mandate, because I've never given those. I think anyone who does so begins to form an occult society. However, there are rules that we all must live by, customs and laws of the land: *You don't ever hurt another human being with motive or malice. You love God, and do good deeds for humankind.* This is universal.

Now, to get back to this ticklish issue: I don't believe in funerals, but I *do* believe in tributes, or even a memorial service. This experience does nothing for those who have passed. If it makes *you* feel better, then by all means, do it. But think about why you need a stainless-steel waterproof coffin. The dead are certainly not going to drown. We, as Gnostics, believe that you can cremate as long as you wait three days. Why three days? It's easier for the orientation of the soul to release from the body.

I keep my father's ashes and a picture of him in my

office. Is he there? No, but it makes me feel better. I went to my beloved Grandmother Ada's funeral when I was 18, and two days later, I went to my truly saintly uncle's funeral. At that point, I said to myself, *This is not right. I want to remember them as they were, not as waxen figures.* Funerals strain the family to the breaking point financially and otherwise. When Daddy died, we had a service and everyone got up and told stories about him. I knew he loved that. It was a celebration of a life, and the lives he had touched.

People are afraid of what others will think, but people eventually think whatever they want anyway. So you have to keep pace to your own drummer.

Now it's time to be better to yourself than you have ever been before. As Nancy says, we want to shut the world out, and we all have our own individual ways of dealing with grief. The only wrong way to go about this process is to give up. So, use *anything* or *anyone* to hang on to your life raft in this endless sea of pain.

Realizations

Today I will try to convert my grief into a positive forward motion. I will use it to give solace to someone else in need.

Time on Earth is temporary and passing. I will make the best of each day until we are reunited with God.

Notes for Reflection

_____

_____

_____

_____

_____

_____

_____

_____

_____

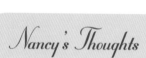 

Nancy's Thoughts

I, too, agree that a funeral is a ritual, much of it for the benefit of those left behind. Some of the significance, though, belongs to the memory of the person who has died. It was important for Daddy and me to give my mother the funeral that was a traditional rite of passage in her family. This was very painful for us, yet releasing as well. It was our final gathering for her, and it was done with the dignity that my mother fought her illness with. She even gave us some specific wishes for her funeral; the rest was up to us.

I wrote and delivered my mother's eulogy at her funeral mass in the company of family and friends. It was very important to me to give my mother that tribute. I knew she would have loved what I said and would have been proud of me. Now I also recognize that I am using the word _me_ in describing reasons for her funeral. It comes as no surprise that it _was_ for me, my father, my brother, my husband, and all our family and friends. Still, I never forget that it may have been *for us*, but it was *about Mom*.

When Daddy died, it was up to me to plan his funeral alone. In character, he left it up to me to figure it all out. He loved teaching me life's lessons. He believed that you learned and grew by doing. Perhaps this final blow of losing my remaining parent made his funeral even more important to me. It was my very last chance to honor my father and mother again in relation to him.

You see, my father and I did not always have as smooth a parent-child relationship as Mom and I did. He and I locked horns more often than not. We both share the characteristic of being stubborn and opinionated. After Mom died, Daddy got softer, but when he began to be physically compromised, his physical pain was compounded by his emotional pain and longing for my mother. One minute he was soft and gentle, and the next, impatient and upset. I understand now that much of that was due to physical as well as emotional pain, and the fact that he had always been a strong and proud man but was now becoming dependent on his daughter.

So when Daddy died, I felt that I owed it to him and myself to help his friends and family understand who the person he kept guarded inside really was. That is why I also wrote and delivered his eulogy. It was as much for him as it was for me.

The worst part about my father's funeral was that I *did* hope it would give me a sense of closure, since I was not with him at the time of his death. I was hoping that if I did a good job on his funeral and the music and flowers and so on, that he would be proud of me and forgive me for not being with him when I had promised I would.

Well, it helped me only minimally there. I'm still working on the guilt of not keeping that promise to my father. This is just part of my intricate lesson with grief and grieving.

Now the other thing that I do regularly is visit the grave sites of my grandparents, my great-grandmother, one uncle, and both my parents, which all happen to be at the same cemetery. If you don't think that's a tough day, think again!

When my dad was alive, we would go together and bring flowers. When my mother was alive, Daddy and Mom would do it. And before that, my grandmother went with my mother, and on and on.

So you see, this is also a tradition. I know that my family is not living inside their burial sites, and I am sure my parents knew that, too. It is just a public sign of remembrance and respect in honor of our ancestors. When my dad and I would go to the cemetery together, he would always point out the grave sites that had flowers, saying that the relatives and friends obviously honored their deceased loved ones.

I promised him I would carry on this tradition. Taking time one day every couple of months to bring flowers is symbolic of my devotion to my relatives. It's one of those things that makes me sad, yet it also makes me feel good that I'm doing it.

I must admit that I talk to my parents while I'm cooking in the kitchen, gardening, or driving in the car. I don't just wait to go to their grave sites. But I think that whatever people do for whatever reasons is just fine, if it's an important part of their grieving process.

Realization

I realize that my grief is selfish, so I will try and force myself to know that my loved ones are happy, and released from their veil of tears.

Notes for Reflection

_____
_____
_____
_____
_____
_____
_____
_____
_____
_____
_____
_____
_____
_____
_____
_____
_____
_____
_____

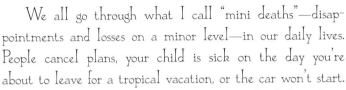

Sylvia's Thoughts

We all go through what I call "mini deaths"—disappointments and losses on a minor level—in our daily lives. People cancel plans, your child is sick on the day you're about to leave for a tropical vacation, or the car won't start.

We learn to cope with these "mini deaths" without even knowing it. When the death of a loved one occurs, some of our coping abilities derived from these "mini deaths" may give us enough strength to go on temporary autopilot for a short time. After that, we're on an expedition to a new realm of emotion and pain.

Standing by my father's bed was the hardest. My spirit guide had warned me that this would be wrenching for me, but I had no concept of how truly difficult it would be. Grief is no stranger to my door. I'd lost a grandmother, an uncle who was a lifeline, a foster son, and on it went. But my daddy, my beloved friend, my best audience, my confidant, was slipping away.

So what if he was 87. People mentioned his age as if it was going to be easy to say, "Okay, you're old, now go Home." I stood at his bedside wishing I could turn back time. I looked at his hands, the very hands that had held mine. He was so lucid, so full of knowledge and memories. We knew that this was our last talk. We talked for six or seven hours straight until he couldn't stand the pain anymore. He beseechingly asked me to get a doctor to give him more pain medication. We both knew what that meant.

He would soon go below the surface of consciousness so the body could relax and the soul could exit. I told him to look for the tunnel and that Jesus was waiting. He nodded and smiled and said, "Sylvia, you look so tired. Go get some water or coffee."

Half crazed, I thought that maybe I would, since my eyes burned and my throat felt as if I had swallowed razor blades. I started to walk out of the room and got to the door, but then I said to myself, "You idiot. You know better. People often push their loved ones away before they go under." I rushed back to the bed. He was unconscious. I hadn't said my last good-bye.

For a moment I was almost caught in that so-often quoted guilt trap, obsessing and struggling with the feeling that "I should have known." I am never psychic about myself, but with my knowledge, couldn't I have stayed a few minutes longer? But I stopped that thought process dead in its tracks. First, we don't have the motive to not be there or arrive on time; we're motivated to do the right thing. But what we must know is that our loved ones understand this. No one carries any remorse, anger, or hurt on the Other Side. No one cares what you do with the car, the house, the jewelry, or what casket or headstone they have. That's for *us;* it's to make *us* feel better. Think about it—if they're up there upset, then it's not heaven, and that's so wrong.

Did I keep talking to my dad? Of course I did, and still do. I talk to all of them who have passed, and so should you. Whether you do it out loud or put it in this journal, they will hear it and know it. They are all around us, and they will communicate with you in one form or another. Trust and be open, listen and learn. Missing our loved ones who have moved forward to the Other Side is a natural human state of emotion, if you have truly known love. Love is selfless, but it makes us vulnerable to pain of many types, grief being one. So what if your grief is self-ish? Is that wrong? Of course not. What would it say about us if we didn't miss our loved ones, didn't grieve, and didn't feel that a part of us was missing? It would mean that we hadn't loved or been able to feel, and then we would be bitter and cold. As is oftentimes quoted because it has such truth, Lord Tennyson said, "'Tis better to have loved and lost, than never to have loved at all."

Each love, each pain, each grief, each joy, hones the soul to perfection for God. The steel is nothing until it has been put into the flame and beaten into shape. So goes life: Through the fire comes the tempered steel that forms our soul and makes us a better temple for God.

Exercise

This is more of an active exercise. Put a chair in the middle of the room. Put a white candle on the floor in front of the chair, a white candle to the left of the chair, one on the right, and also one white candle behind the chair.

Sit in the chair and ask for God's grace and for the white light to surround you. Ask that these candles be symbols of enlightenment. Ask your loved one to cross into this circle of light and give you a sign. It may be a smell of flowers, a breeze on your face, or, like what happened to a mother I know who lost her young son, a light kiss on her nose. Be sure that there's no draft in the room, and you may even see the candle flames dance or go out.

There are myriad ways in which entities come through—too many to list here—so I'm just going to list the most common ones:

* The phone rings, but no one is there. It's not even a dial tone; it's just a dead line.

* The scent of flowers, lavender, lilac, roses, cologne, or the smell of pipe tobacco (like my dad's cherry-blend pipe tobacco).

* Moving objects—that is, putting something down and having it appear somewhere else. You might even test this one.

* Buzzing in the ears or a muted feeling in the ears, when for a minute or two you feel as if you're in a dream.

* The dropping of coins. Finding the coins everywhere, the car, the yard, and all over the house; or finding more coins than usual.

* Waking up at the same time every night—for example, 3:15 A.M. or 4:30 A.M. The reason for this is that the atmosphere in the room changes, and your subconscious is aware of it.

* Different electrical disturbances. After loved ones have passed, lights may flicker, or the TV may go on and off.

* Footsteps; cold spots; a hand on your face, arm, leg, or shoulder; the feeling that someone is sitting on the bed or in the room with you.

* Spirit animals who also make their presence known by rubbing against your leg or nuzzling you.

* Spirits coming in, in what may appear to be a dream, but what seems almost too real to be one. Then they will either smile or tell you they're all right, or many times give you messages.

* A loud rapping sound in the middle of the room, much like a firecracker or clap. Not unlike thunder, but on a larger scale.

No matter what you feel, it's always important to say, "If you come from God, you are welcome, but if not, go to the light of the Holy Spirit." This is not to imply that people who have passed over are ever evil, but they may simply be lost or Earthbound spirits, and you don't want them to attach themselves to you. As many people as I have spoken to who have passed, whether a ghost (Earthbound) or a spirit, I've never acquired any hangers-on, so to speak. There is nothing on the Other Side that can ever hurt you. You have to worry about life here on Earth—that's where the evil lies. But even then, armed with your tools of protection—such as faith, love, and compassion—nothing can really harm you.

Most people make it to the Other Side, but just for good measure, I always say to deceased loved ones to let them go, "I will not hold on to you. Go to God, and we will be fine." This is a way to let them go through the tunnel and meet all *their* loved ones. Then you can be assured that you've helped them to make the transition. Once they're over on the Other Side, talk to them and ask them for advice. You'll be amazed by how much power spirits have after they've passed. I've even gotten warnings to give to loved ones, advice and consolation, and validation, which in and of itself provides comfort.

Notes for Reflection

_____

_____

_____

_____

_____

_____

_____

_____

_____

Nancy's Thoughts

A woman I know, whom I'll call Sue, is dealing with the suicide of her husband. As I've talked with her, I've been made aware that there are many people who have lived through the nightmare of losing a loved one by their own hand. The subject is not often addressed. Perhaps it makes people uncomfortable.

After listening to Sue's story, though, *I'm* more comfortable. I'm also grateful that she shared her experience with me so that it could be discussed. As I've learned through her eyes and her children's eyes, suicide brings an extra load to carry through the journey of grief.

Sue explained that there were thousands of times when her husband decided *not* to take his own life. She said that he lived in a tortured world. He tried different medications, some of which were very helpful, and some not so helpful.

Sue was aware of her husband's dark side, and in the back of her mind, she always wondered *when*, not *if*, he would take his own life. Yet in her grief, Sue felt understanding about his emotional illness. She said that it was as if he had been terminally ill. She did not feel that he did this *to* her or their children, but essentially *for* himself, and in a smaller way, for his family, possibly thinking that they would be better off without his pain.

Sue has come a long way with hard work, support groups, and through helping others in the same situation. She has noted that as a widow of a spouse who has chosen suicide, she personally never felt ashamed, but she has met many others who do. Shame seems to be an added stage for many in this situation.

Sue has become strong in her conviction to move forward for herself and her children. While her husband was alive, he often encouraged her to go on with her life if he were to leave. She explained that in sharing a life with someone, you discuss your dreams, goals, and future plans for yourself and your children. And in the wake of your partner committing suicide, your tendency is to continue on with those same plans and dreams—partly for the person who has passed on, and also for yourself and your kids. Sue speaks openly about her experience and holds her head high, but it has never been an easy road. The demands and challenges she faces as a woman and a mother are constantly being confronted, and are sometimes linked back to that one moment in time when her husband made that fateful choice.

Now it has been about three years since her husband's death, and Sue is just starting to fix up the house and get her physical surroundings in order. Up until now, she did not even want to fix a doorknob, because she resented that that used to be her husband's job. Even after three years, though, she sometimes feels like it has only been about three days. This I can personally relate to myself.

※ ※ ※

To further explore the feelings of those left behind, I spoke with the son of a man who chose suicide. This boy, whom I'll call Craig, was forthcoming and wanted to share his feelings about his father.

Children are amazing, and have insights that provide a continual education for me. I learned that Craig was not angry that his father died at his own hand, but his anger resulted from the fact that he didn't know that his father was struggling with an emotional illness. He stated that perhaps had he known, he could have talked with his father about his illness and might have been able to change the ultimate outcome.

As we spoke further, it became clear that Craig *did* know that his father probably would have made the same choice whether they had discussed his illness or not. It was also clear that his father's act had forever changed his young life. Still, he bore no negative feelings toward his father; in fact, he expressed great love and gratitude for the time he did have with him. It was wonderful to see that this boy admired both his parents, and was given positive guidance by his mother, who urged him not to feel shame or guilt over what had happened.

At this time, Craig seems far more evolved in his journey than I am. I see how he fills the empty space as best he can with his continued love for his father, and his devotion to, and love for, his mother. He also reaches out to friends and makes them his family, and learns all he can from those he opens his heart to. He still grieves and has milestones to face as part of the grieving process, but he has faith in those he has surrounded himself with. He allows himself to feel whatever he needs to feel at any particular time without self-recrimination. He also doesn't hide from his feelings or from what has happened. He is open and willing to share his experience with pride, and with the anticipation of learning more.

Again, I have gained strength and encouragement from seeing how a child processes grief and learns from it.

Realization

I talk to you from my heart and through my written word, and know that you will reveal your thoughts to me if I listen and watch with the openness and purity of a child.

Notes for Reflection

Sylvia's Thoughts

We profoundly grieve the loss of loved ones who go to the Other Side as a result of suicide or murder, and we are also devastated when children or grandchildren leave us. Certainly, we (temporarily) lose people when they die, but we also feel a great loss when there is a divorce in the family or some similar type of personal crisis. (However, I won't address that type of loss here—I'll discuss that in a subsequent relationship journal.)

Suicide is self-indulgent. It leaves the people behind wondering what they could have done or said to change what has happened. Sometimes the person committing suicide leaves a note for those left behind, but often nothing is left, which leaves those behind even more baffled.

People who commit suicide out of spite come right back in utero and into life to fulfill their original contract with God. They do not pass to the Other Side. It's like a horseshoe effect. They are out of this life and right back in immediately. They are still bound to complete the lessons they contracted to learn.

Most suicides I have studied—and I would venture to say this without hesitation—stem from an actual chemical imbalance in the brain. When this chemical imbalance is left untreated, or when medication does not help, the emotions and negativity drown the intellect, and the person is in so much pain that suicide becomes their only choice. There is no reverberation when suicide occurs under these circumstances.

What we must all understand is that as human beings, we do not have the kind of power or control to change what a person chooses for him- or herself. Suicide is done specifically for the person choosing to leave. It is not *against* anyone, but a choice one person makes in that split second when deciding to end their life.

Those of you who are living through grief because a loved one has committed suicide must not take on guilt or responsibility for the act. This experience is also part of *your* contract with God, and part of your spiritual perfection. There are extra burdens that may come from being a widow, widower, or a parent or child of an individual who has committed suicide, but know that you are a strong soul to have put this in your plan. You will gain strengths and insights that will bring you knowledge and compassion that you will be able to share with others on the same path.

Remember, we are all students, and we are all teachers.

Notes for Reflection
Use this space to record visitations, communications, and dreams from loved ones on the Other Side.

_____

_____

_____

_____

_____

_____

_____

_____

_____

Notes for Reflection

Use this space to write letters to the Universe, to God, and to those on the Other Side.

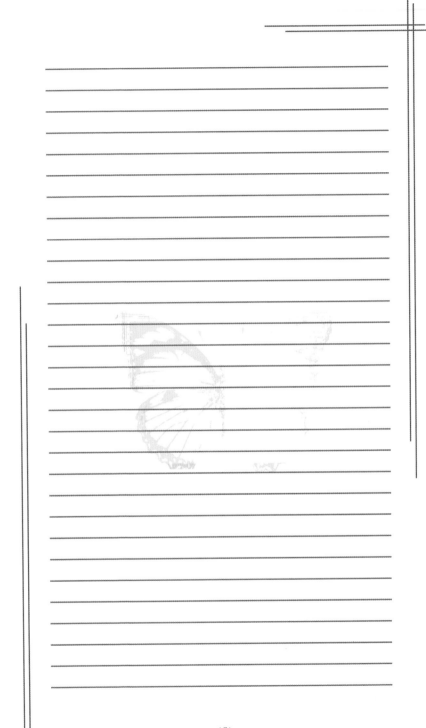

Afterword

It is our hope that this journal has served as your friend, companion, and helpmate as you recorded your thoughts, feelings, letters, and spiritual communications with those who have gone Home. We share the depth of your feelings of loss. We know what it feels like to wake up in the night, alone and frightened, wishing that we could attribute all the pain and heartache to a bad dream—but knowing that it's all too real.

We are so sensitive to each other's feelings of grief that we recognize the look in one another's eyes. Our empathy and understanding has taken us through some very dark moments, and we're sure will continue to do so—as those moments still sneak up on us when we least expect it.

May the rest of *your* days be filled with peace, love, and acceptance—and loving friends and companions who will soothe you in your time of need.

And know that God loves you—*we do!*

— **Sylvia and Nancy**

About the Authors

Nancy Dufresne is a registered nurse with extensive experience in trauma surgery, ICU, labor and delivery, and oncology/hospice nursing. She has been married to Sylvia Browne's oldest son, Paul, for 17 years. Nancy and Paul have one son, Jeffrey, age seven, who is the light of their lives, especially through all of the hard times.

※ ※ ※

Millions of people have witnessed **Sylvia Browne's** incredible psychic powers on TV shows such as *Montel, Larry King Live, Entertainment Tonight,* and *Unsolved Mysteries;* and she has been profiled in *Cosmopolitan, People* magazine, and other national media. Her on-target psychic readings have helped police solve crimes, and she astounds audiences wherever she appears.

Please contact Sylvia at **www.sylvia.org** or: Sylvia Browne Corp., 35 Dillon Ave., Campbell, CA 95008, (408) 379-7070.

Also by Sylvia Browne

Books

Adventures of a Psychic (with Antoinette May)

Astrology Through a Psychic's Eyes

Conversations with the Other Side
   (available October 2001)

God, Creation, and Tools for Life

*Life on the Other Side**

Meditations (available January 2001)

The Nature of Good and Evil (available March 2001)

The Other Side and Back (with Lindsay Harrison)*

Soul's Perfection
            and . . .
My Life with Sylvia Browne
   (by Sylvia's son, Chris Dufresne)

Audio Programs

Adventures of a Psychic (abridged audio book)

Angels and Spirit Guides

Healing the Body, Mind, and Soul

Making Contact with the Other Side

*The Other Side of Life: A Discussion on Death, Dying,
   and the Graduation of the Soul*

Sylvia Browne's Tools for Life

*(The books and audios above can be ordered from Hay House, except for those with an asterisk.)

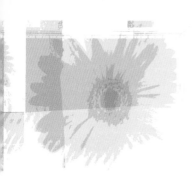

Other Hay House Lifestyles Titles

Flip Books

101 Ways to Happiness, by Louise L. Hay

101 Ways to Health and Healing, by Louise L. Hay

101 Ways to Romance, by Barbara De Angelis, Ph.D.

101 Ways to Transform Your Life, by Dr. Wayne W. Dyer

Books

A Garden of Thoughts, by Louise L. Hay

Aromatherapy A–Z, by Connie Higley, Alan Higley, and Pat Leatham

Aromatherapy 101, by Karen Downes

Colors & Numbers, by Louise L. Hay

Constant Craving A–Z, by Doreen Virtue, Ph.D.

Dream Journal, by Leon Nacson

Healing with Herbs and Home Remedies A–Z, by Hanna Kroeger

Healing with the Angels Oracle Cards (booklet and card pack), by Doreen Virtue, Ph.D.

Healing with the Fairies Oracle Cards (booklet and card pack), by Doreen Virtue, Ph.D.

Heal Your Body A–Z, by Louise L. Hay

Home Design with Feng Shui A–Z, by Terah Kathryn Collins

Homeopathy A–Z, by Dana Ullman, M.P.H.

Inner Wisdom, by Louise L. Hay

Interpreting Dreams A–Z, by Leon Nacson

Natural Gardening A–Z, by Donald W. Trotter

Natural Healing for Dogs and Cats A–Z,
    by Cheryl Schwartz, D.V.M.

Natural Pregnancy A–Z, by Carolle Jean-Murat, M.D.

Pleasant Dreams, by Amy E. Dean

Rose Gardening A–Z, by Donald W. Trotter

Weddings A–Z, by Deborah McCoy

What Color Is Your Personality?,
    by Carol Ritberger, Ph.D.

What Is Spirit?, by Lexie Brockway Potamkin

You Can Heal Your Life, by Louise L. Hay

Affirmation Cards

Power Thought Cards, by Louise L. Hay

Wisdom Cards, by Louise L. Hay

All of the above titles may be ordered by calling Hay House at the numbers on the next page.